Random Acts of Coloring

Volume 1

Coloring books for adults by

Tiffany Schroeder

Welcome to Random Acts of Coloring.

Please like the Facebook page for updates about new books, free samples, giveaways, and coloring contests.

www.facebook.com/RAOColoring

Please remember to place a blank sheet in between the pages, so that if you are using markers, there is no bleed through to the next image.

Copyright 2015

ISBN-13: 978-1511783897

ISBN-10: 1511783893

Front cover colored by – Joni Russell

Back cover colored by – Vady Anderman

Some pieces of art in this book have been adapted from ancient works.

Drawing 2 – adapted from the Indian lotus

Drawing 14 – adapted from the Lindisfarne Gospels, 11th century

Drawing 20 – adapted from the frieze in the main room of the Queen's apartments in Knossos on the island of Crete

Drawing 22 – adapted from the Lindisfarne Gospels, 11th Century

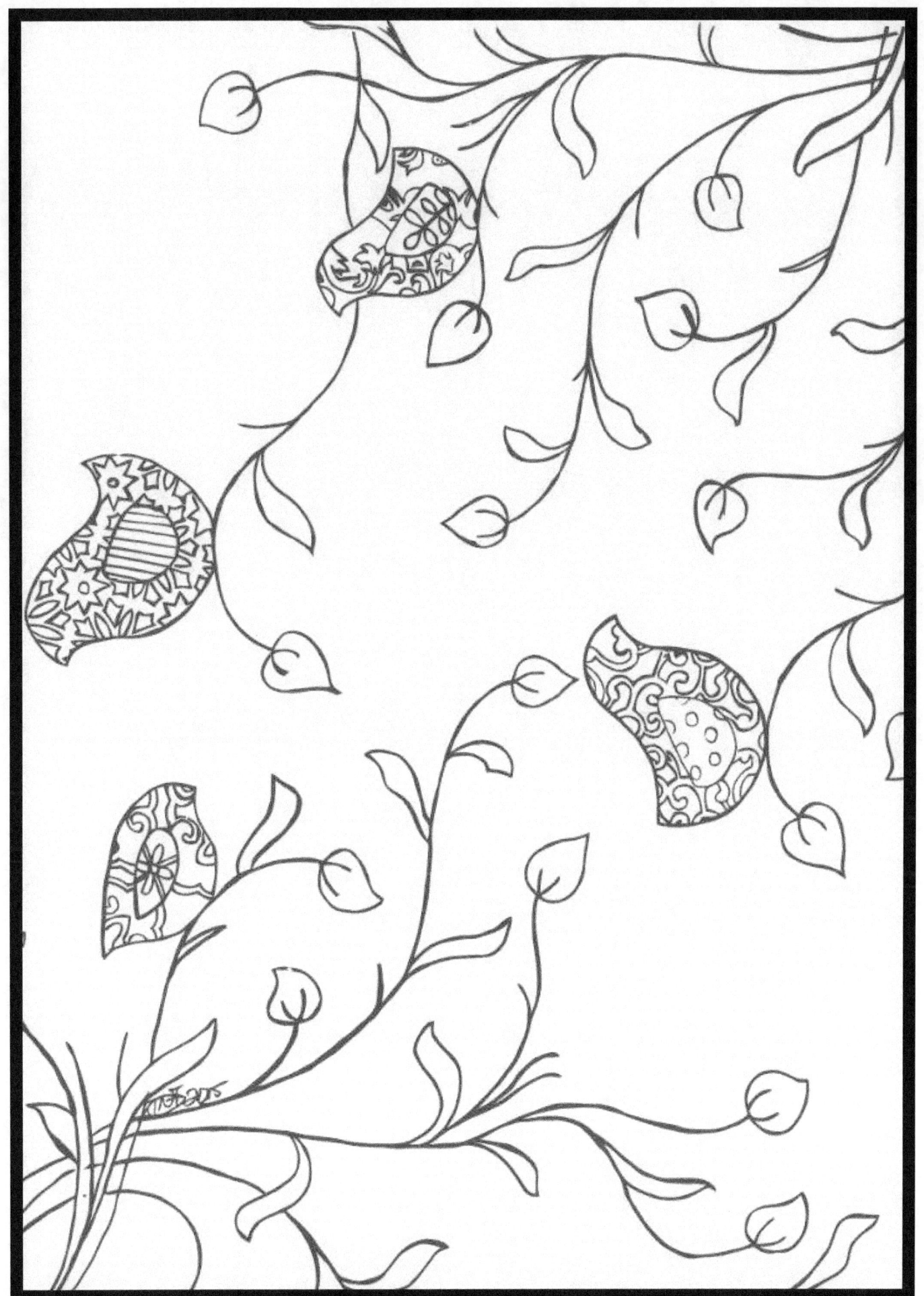

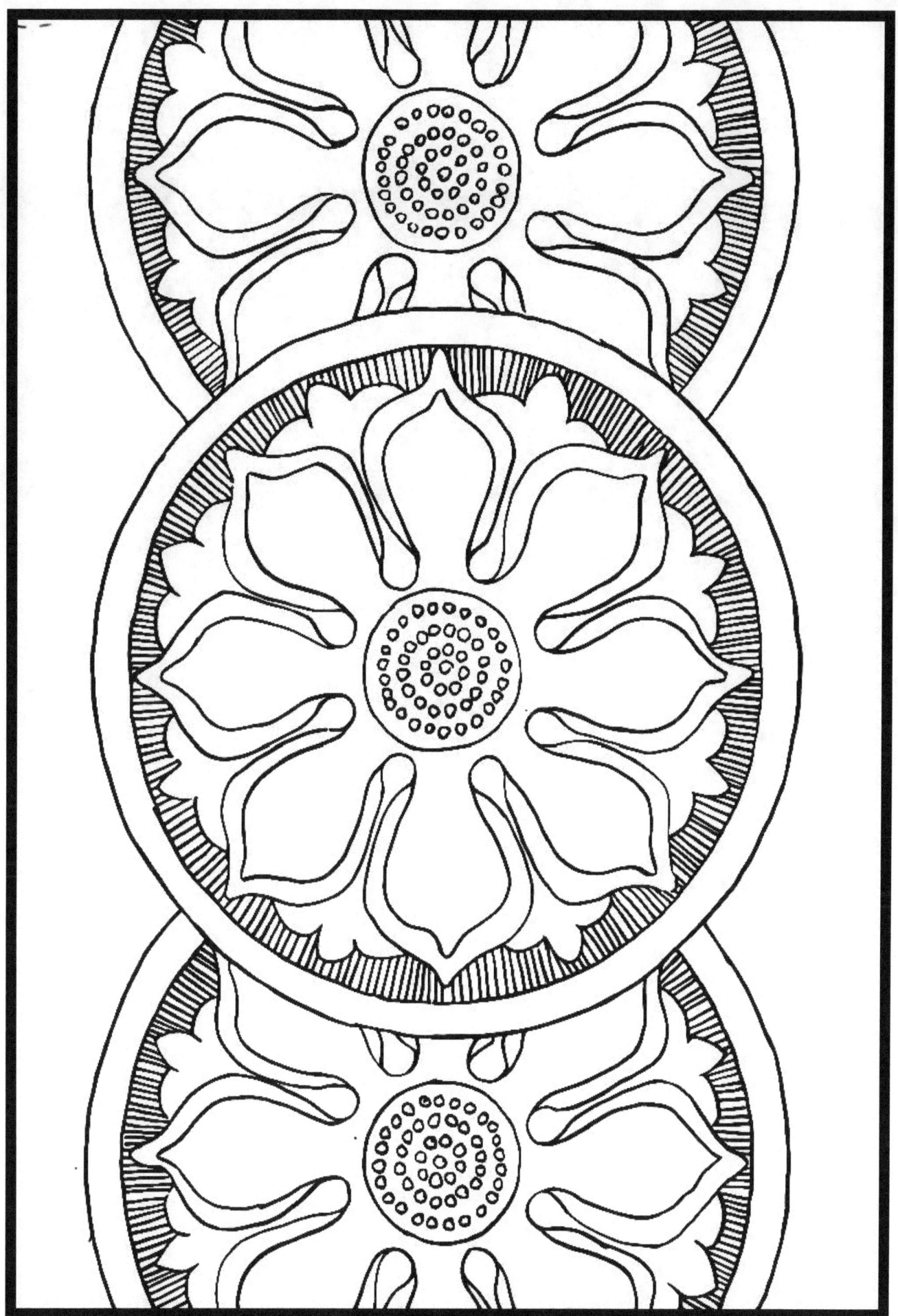

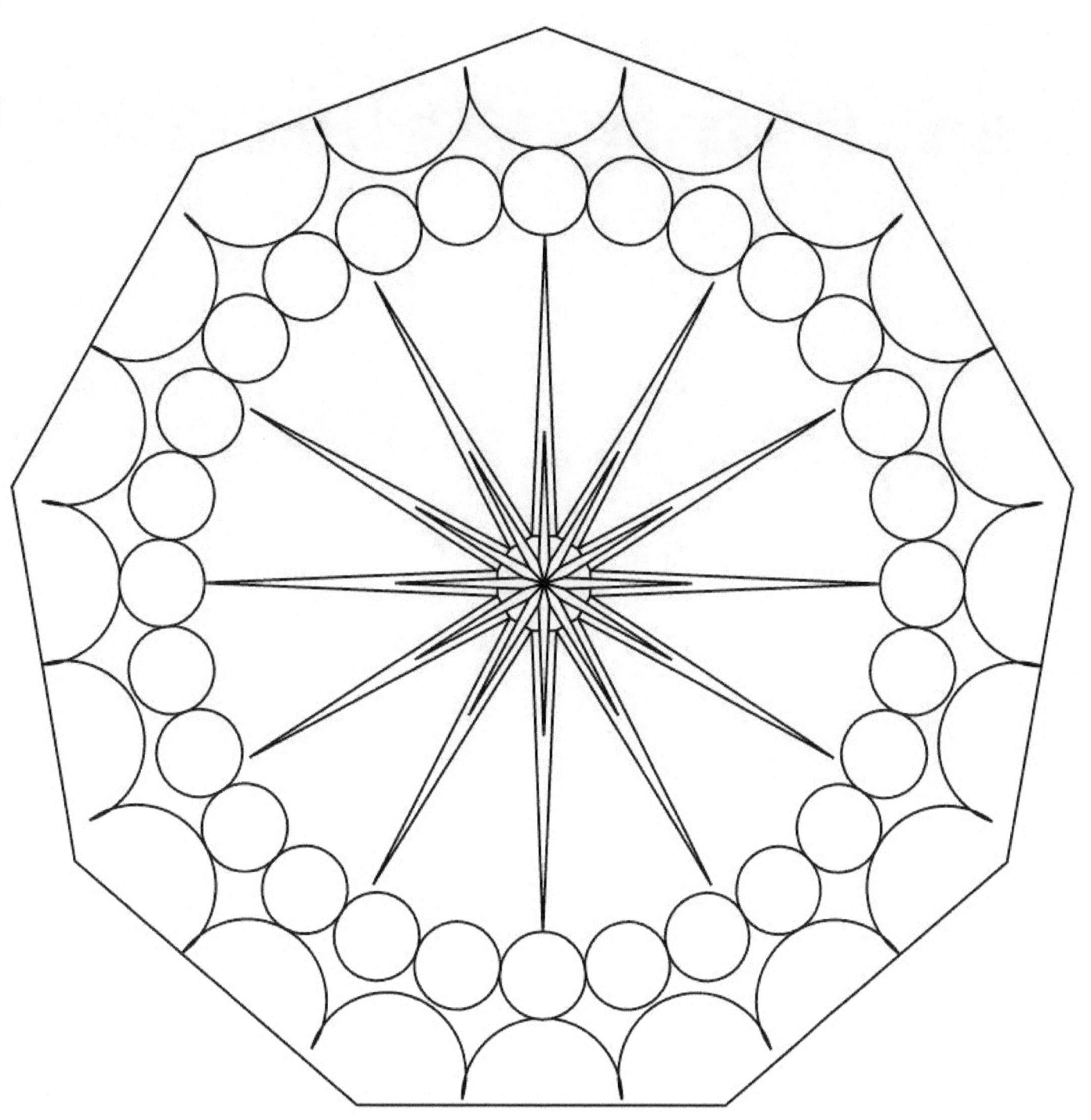

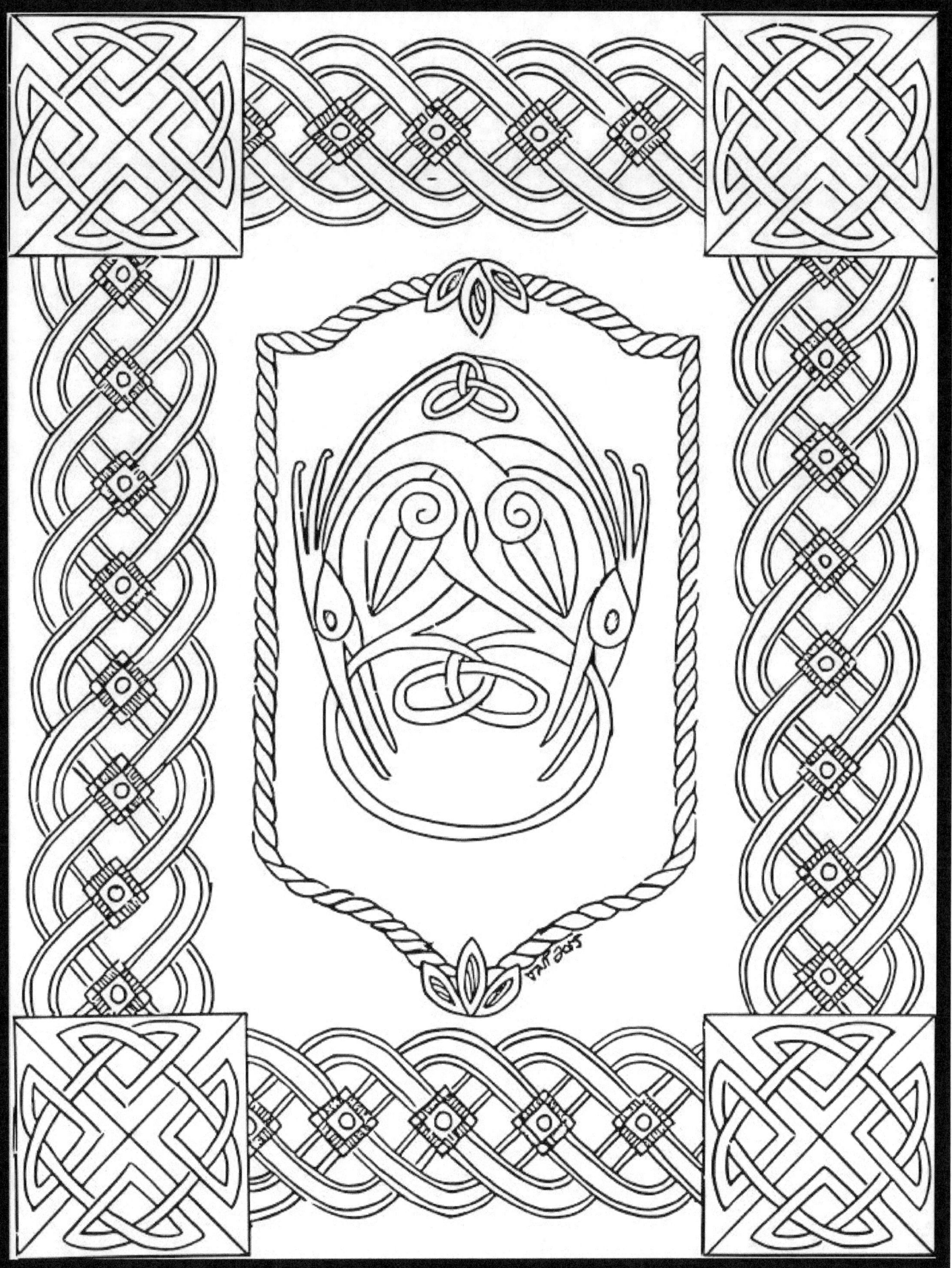

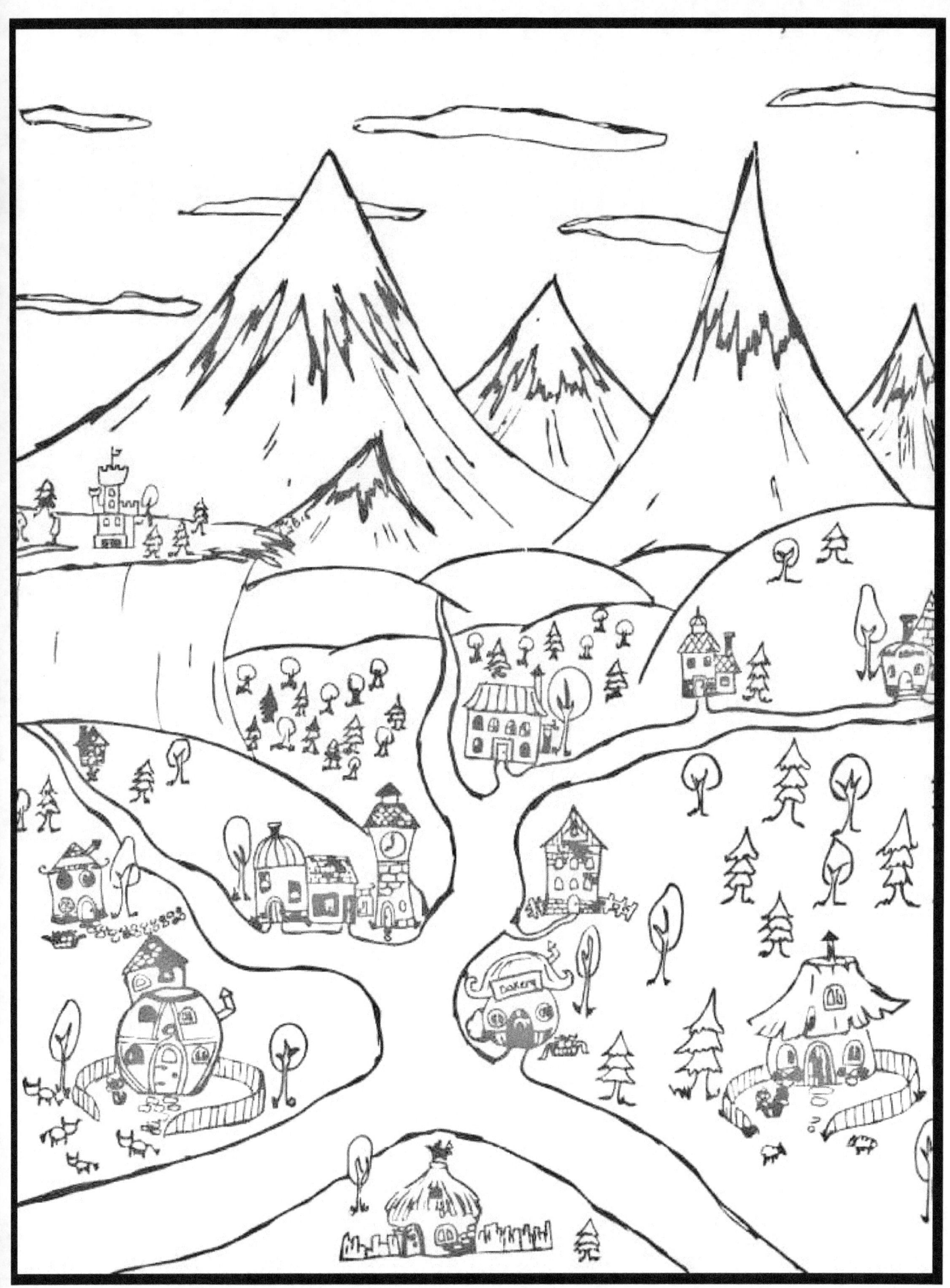

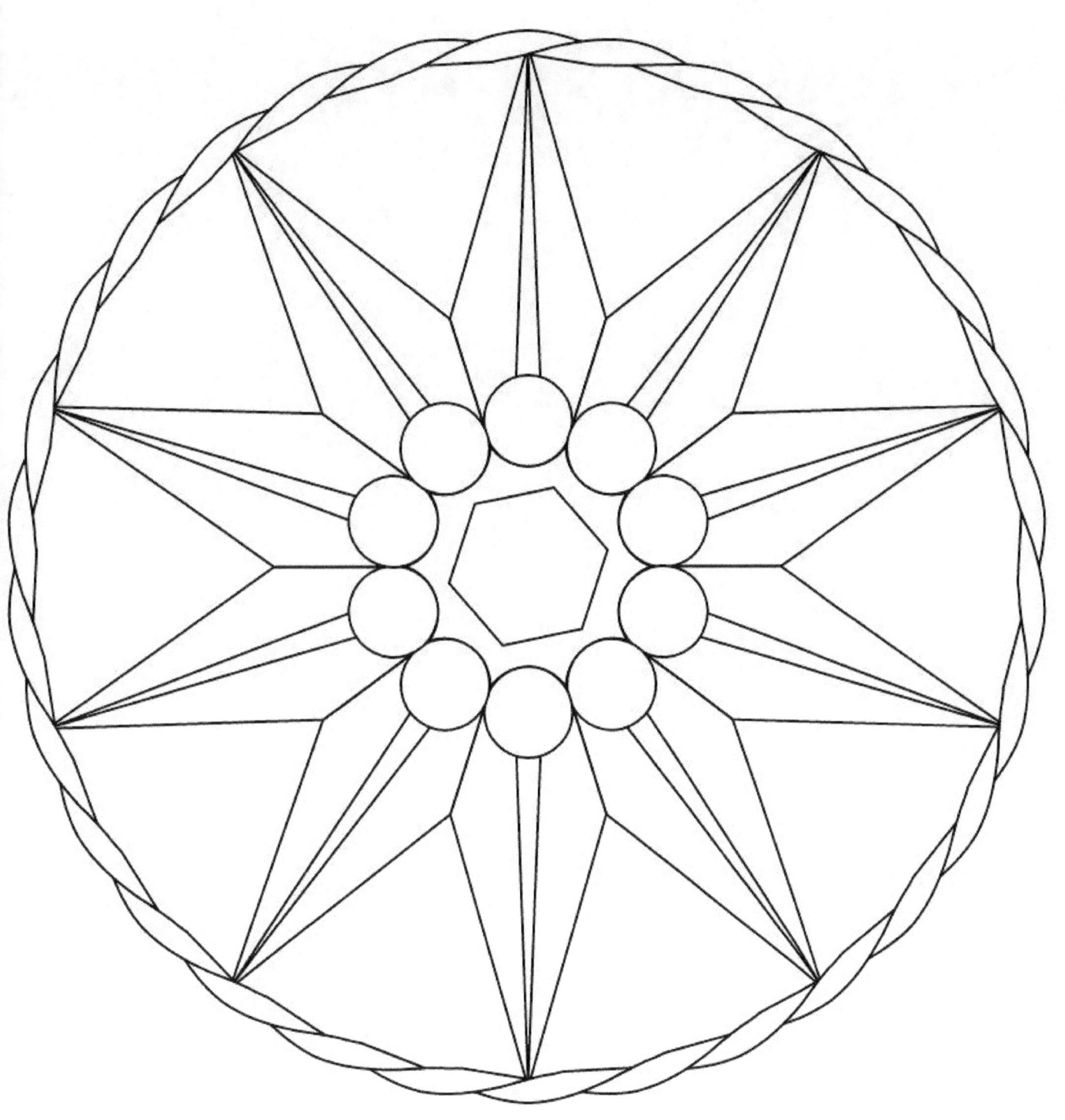

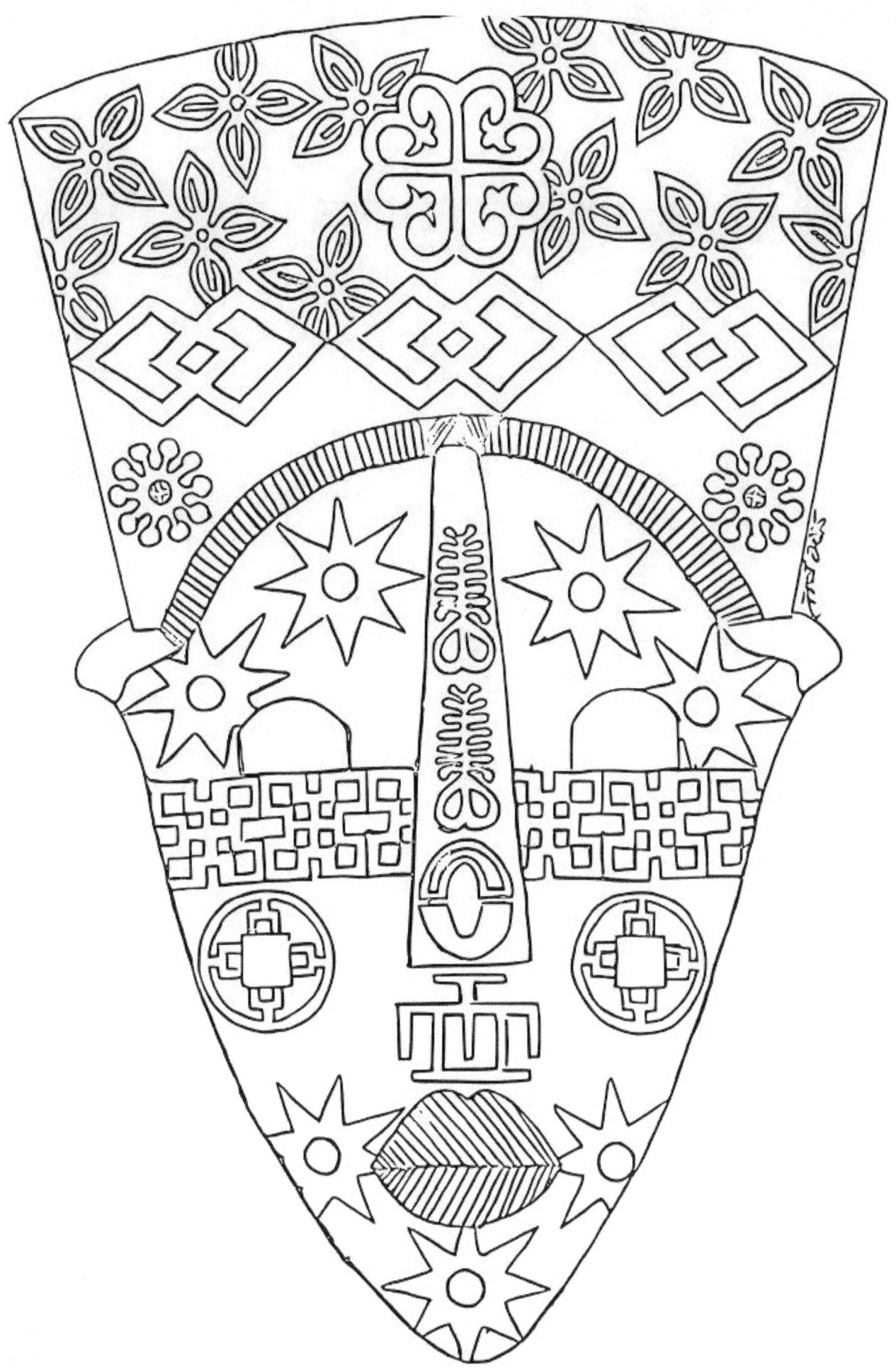

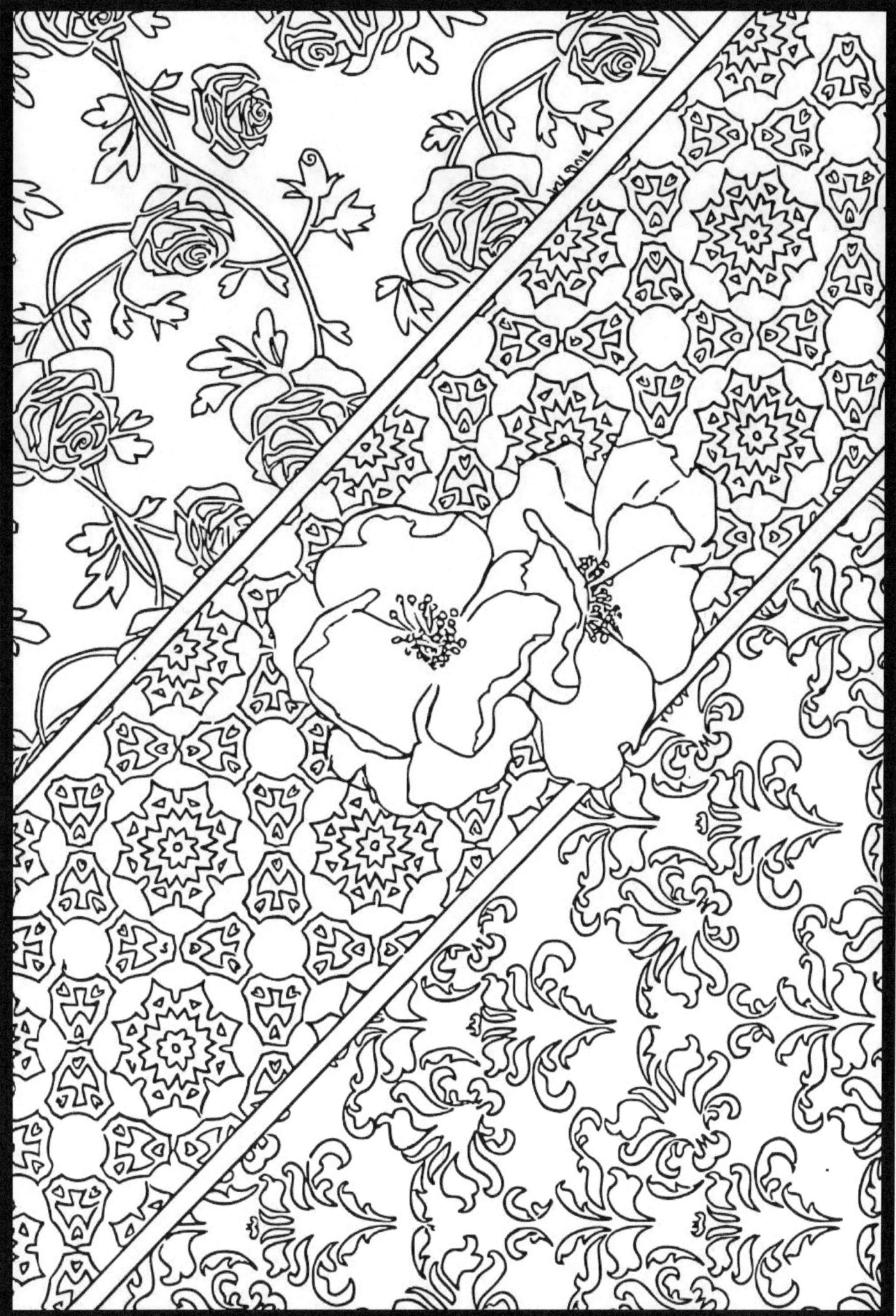

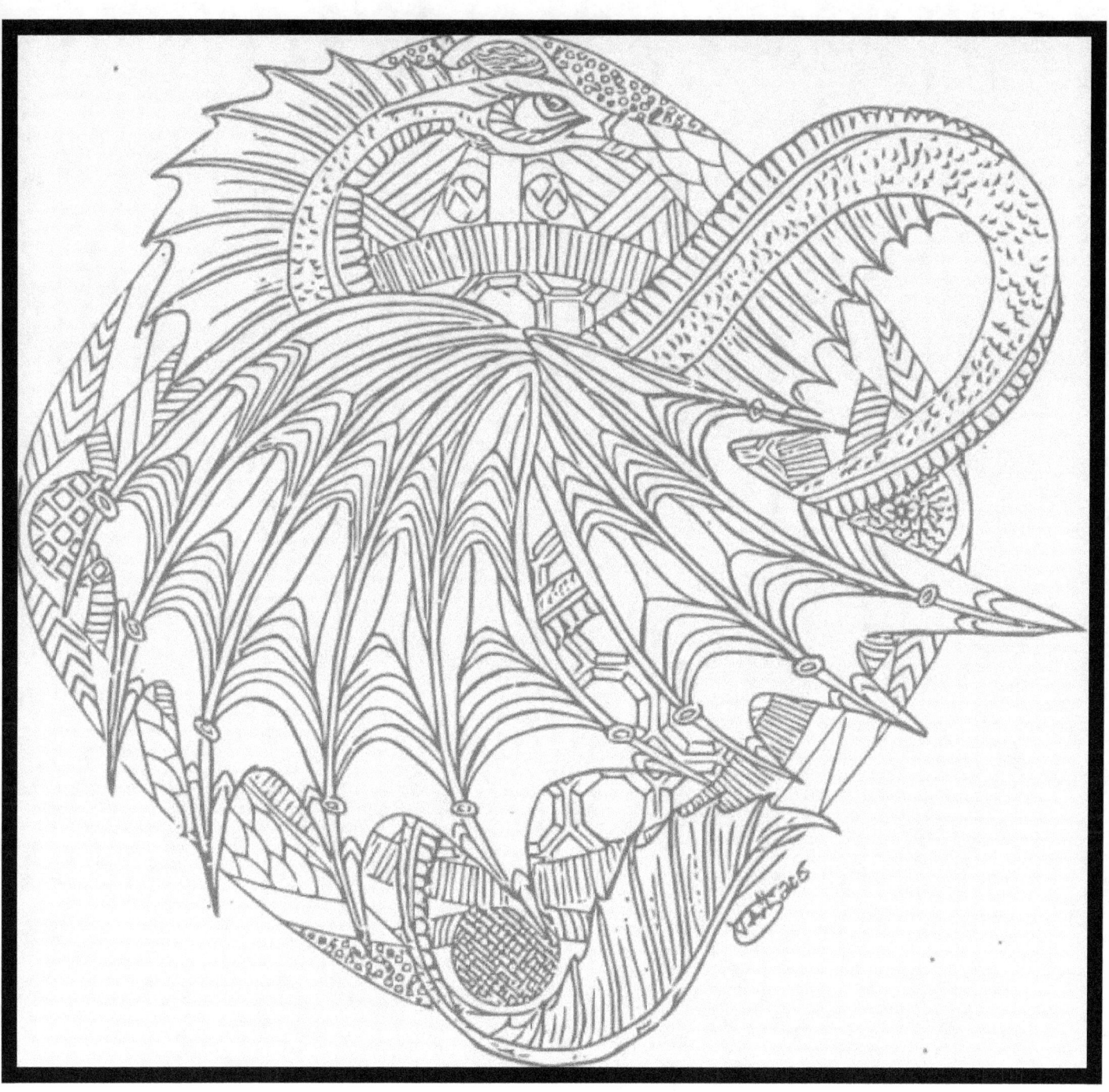

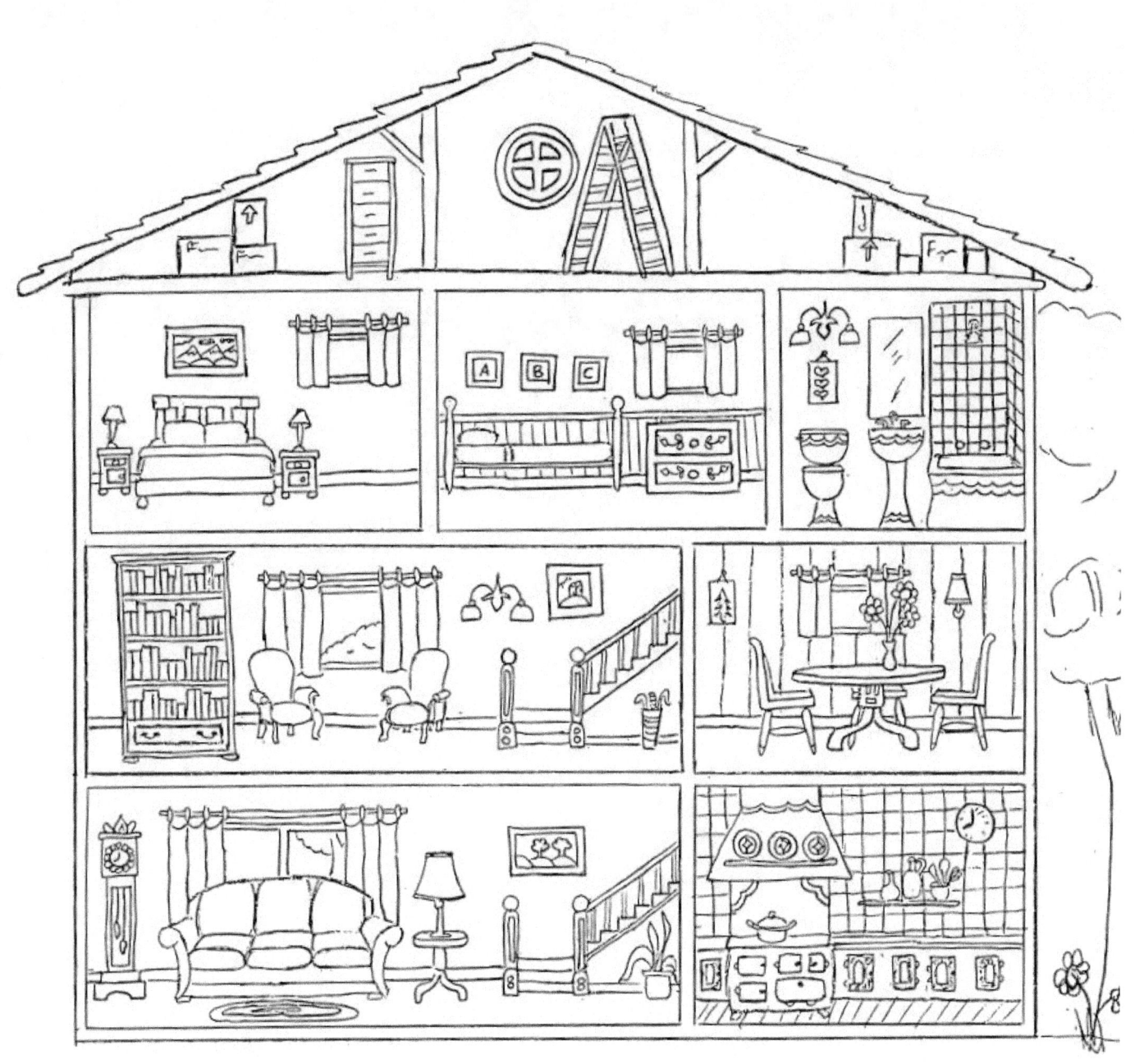

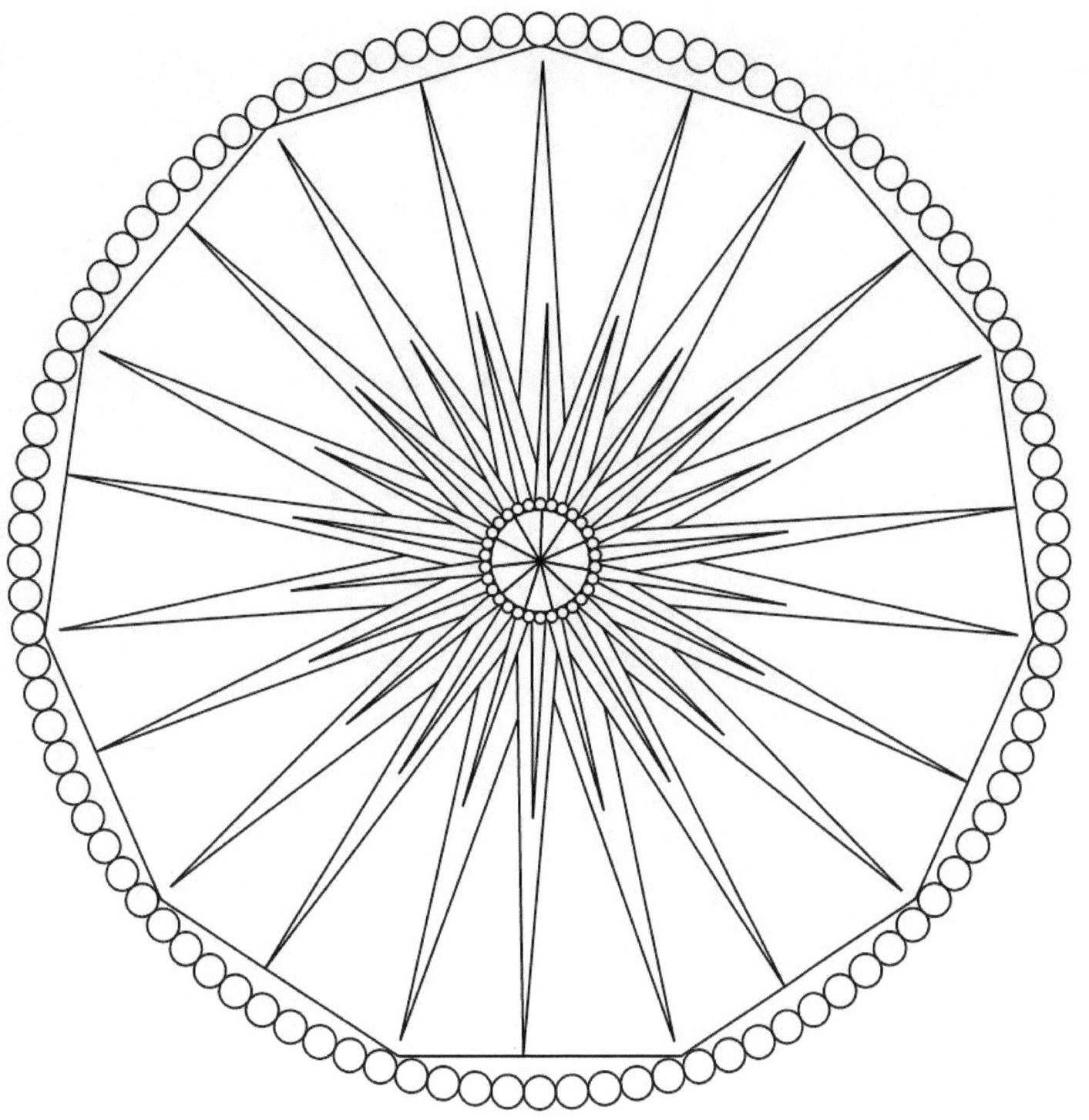

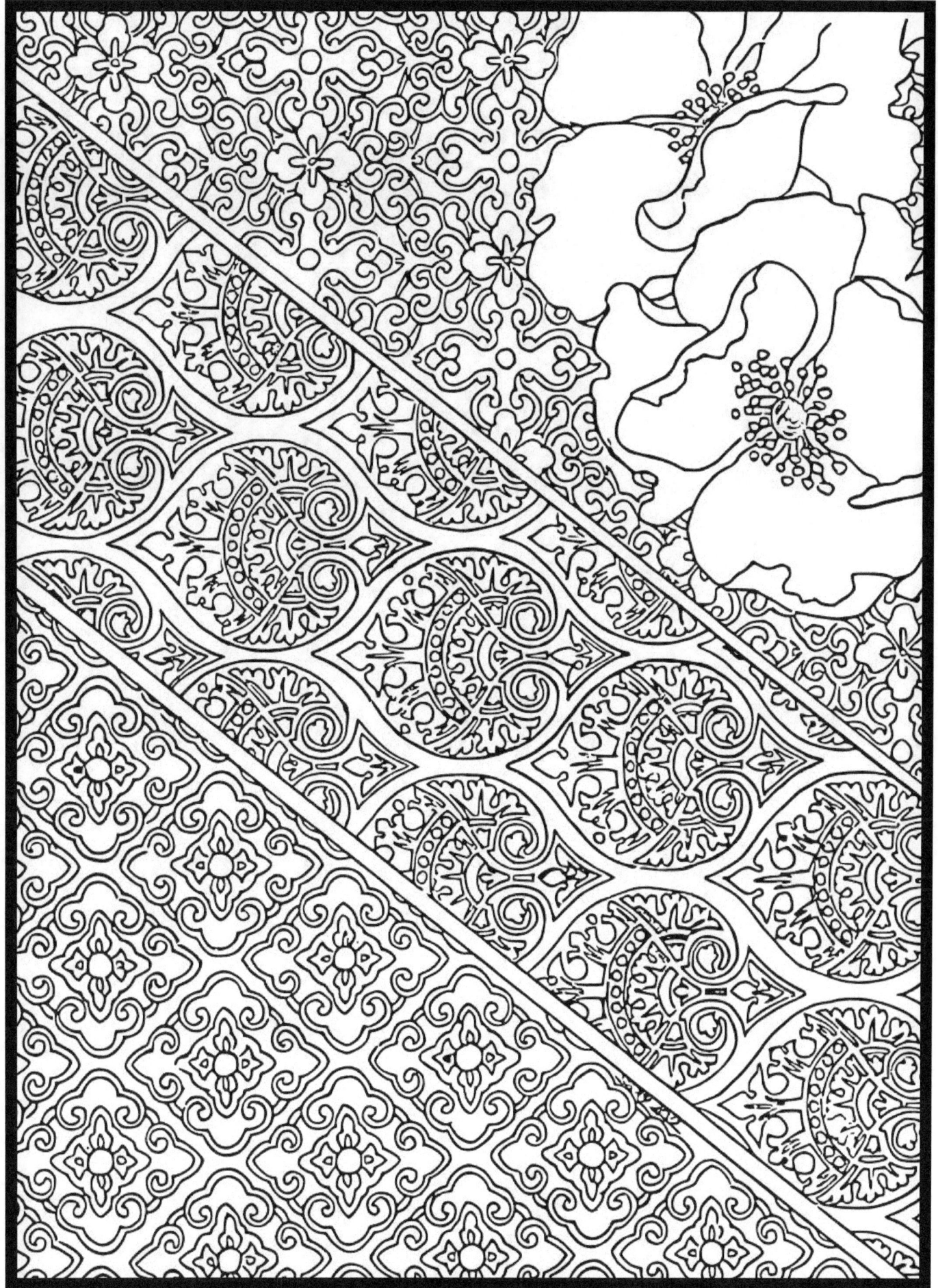

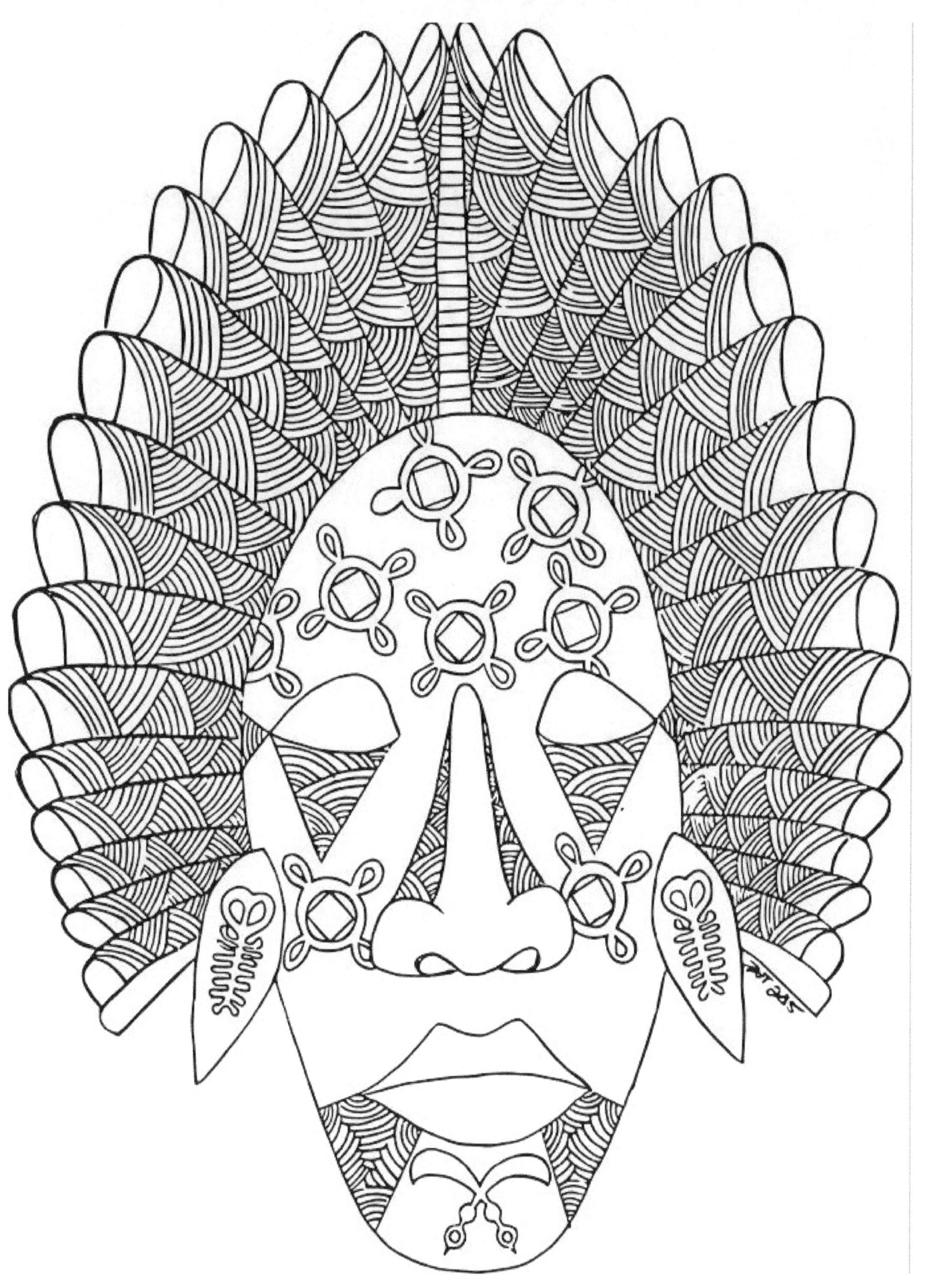

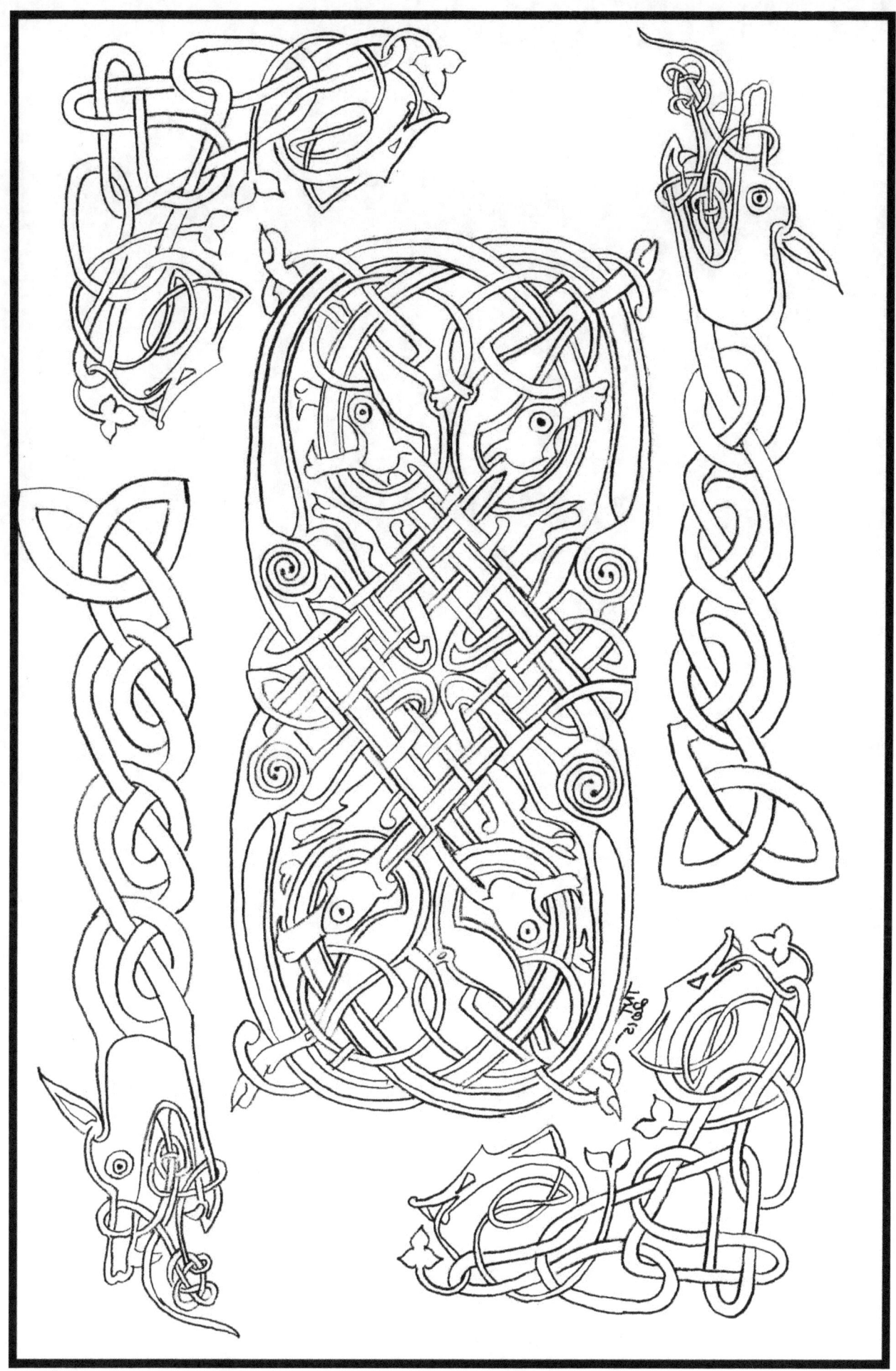

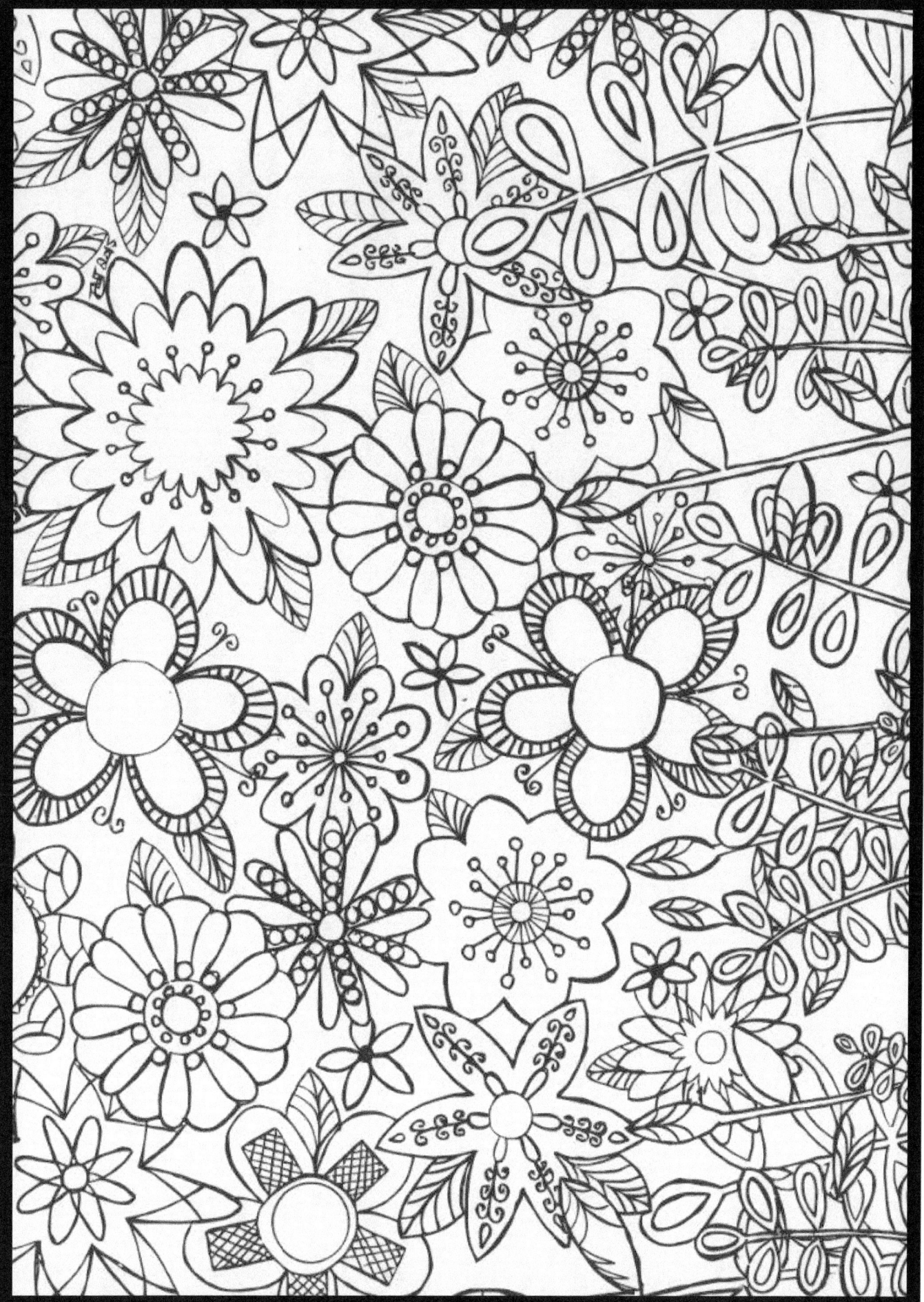

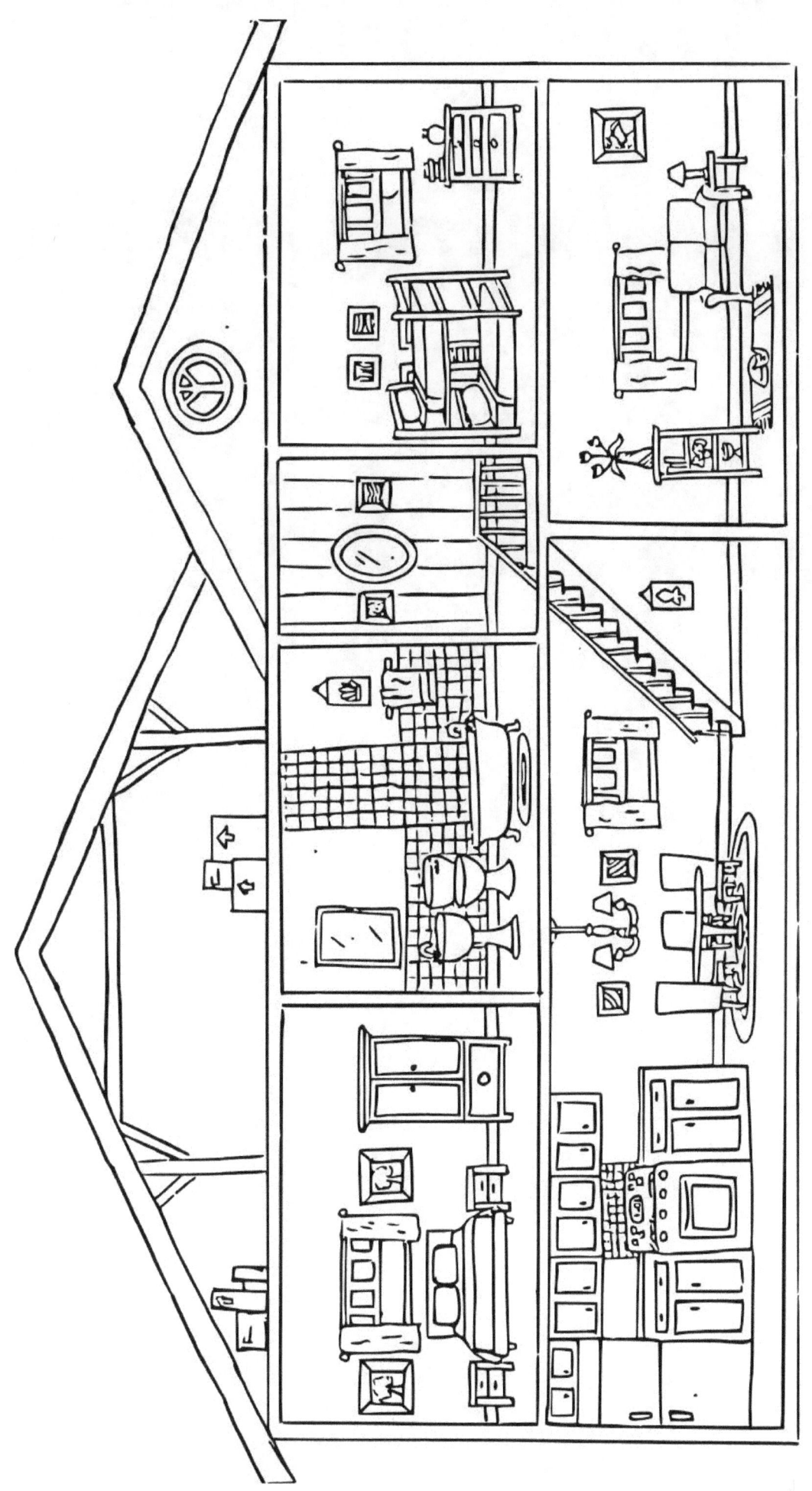

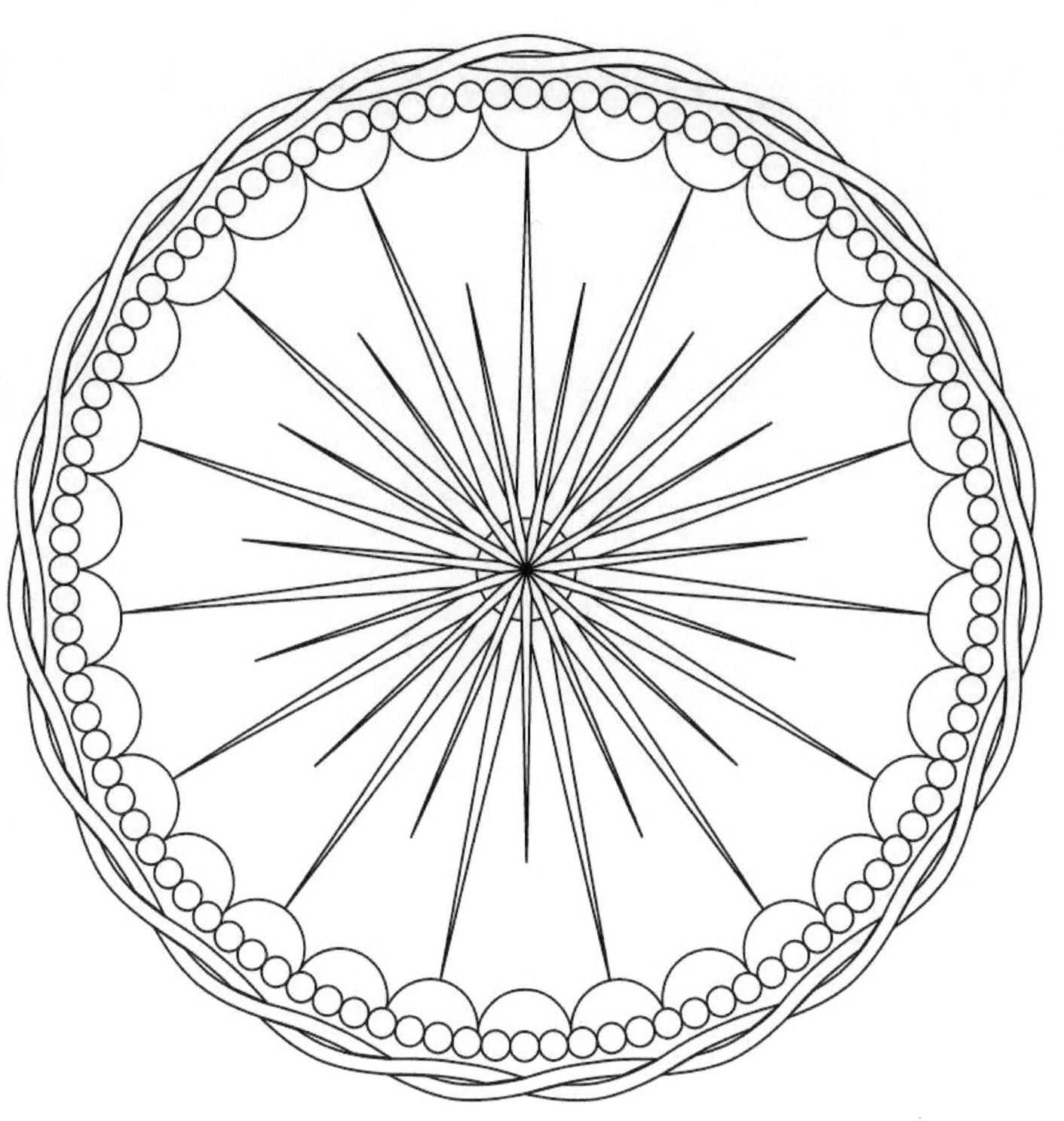

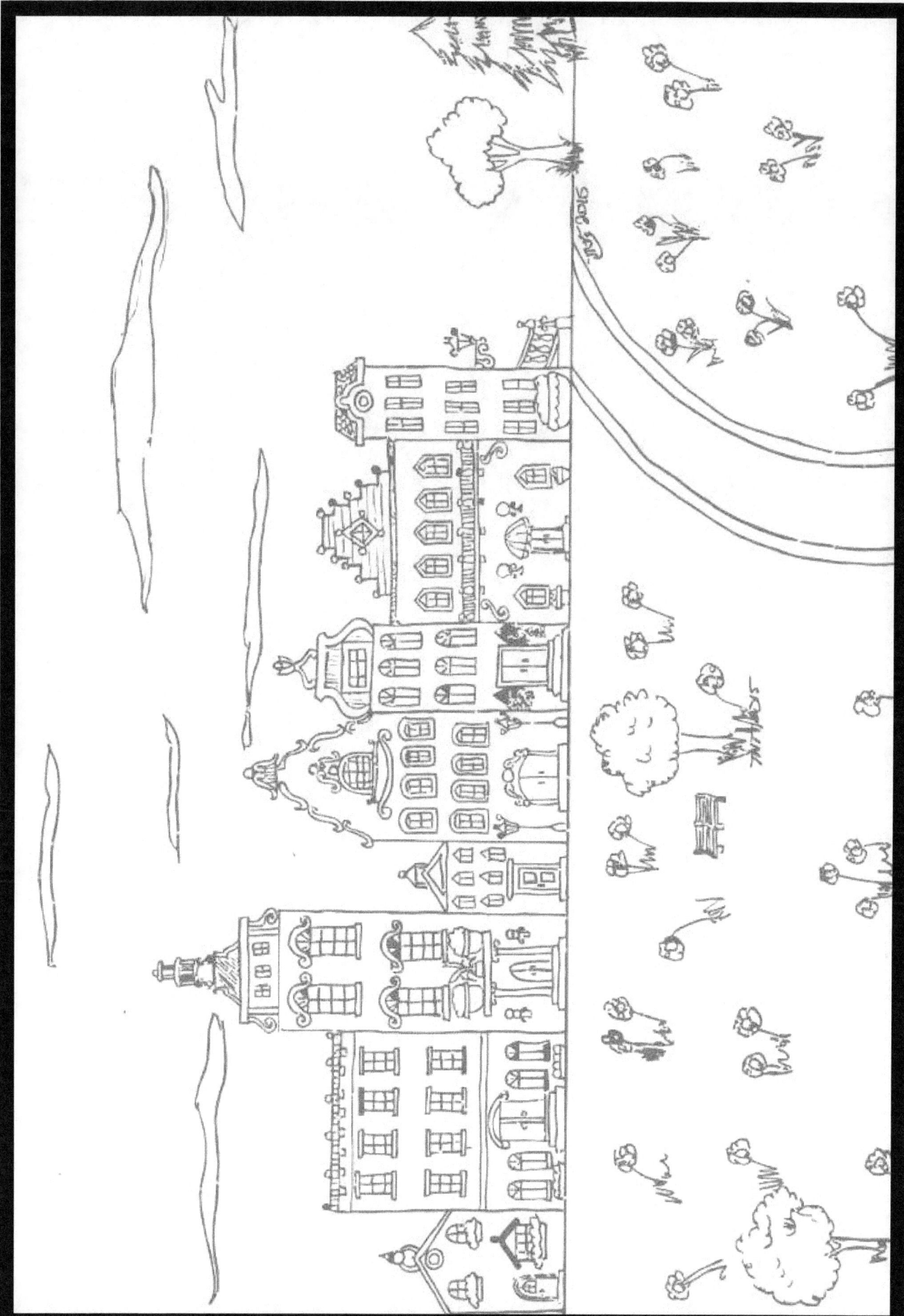

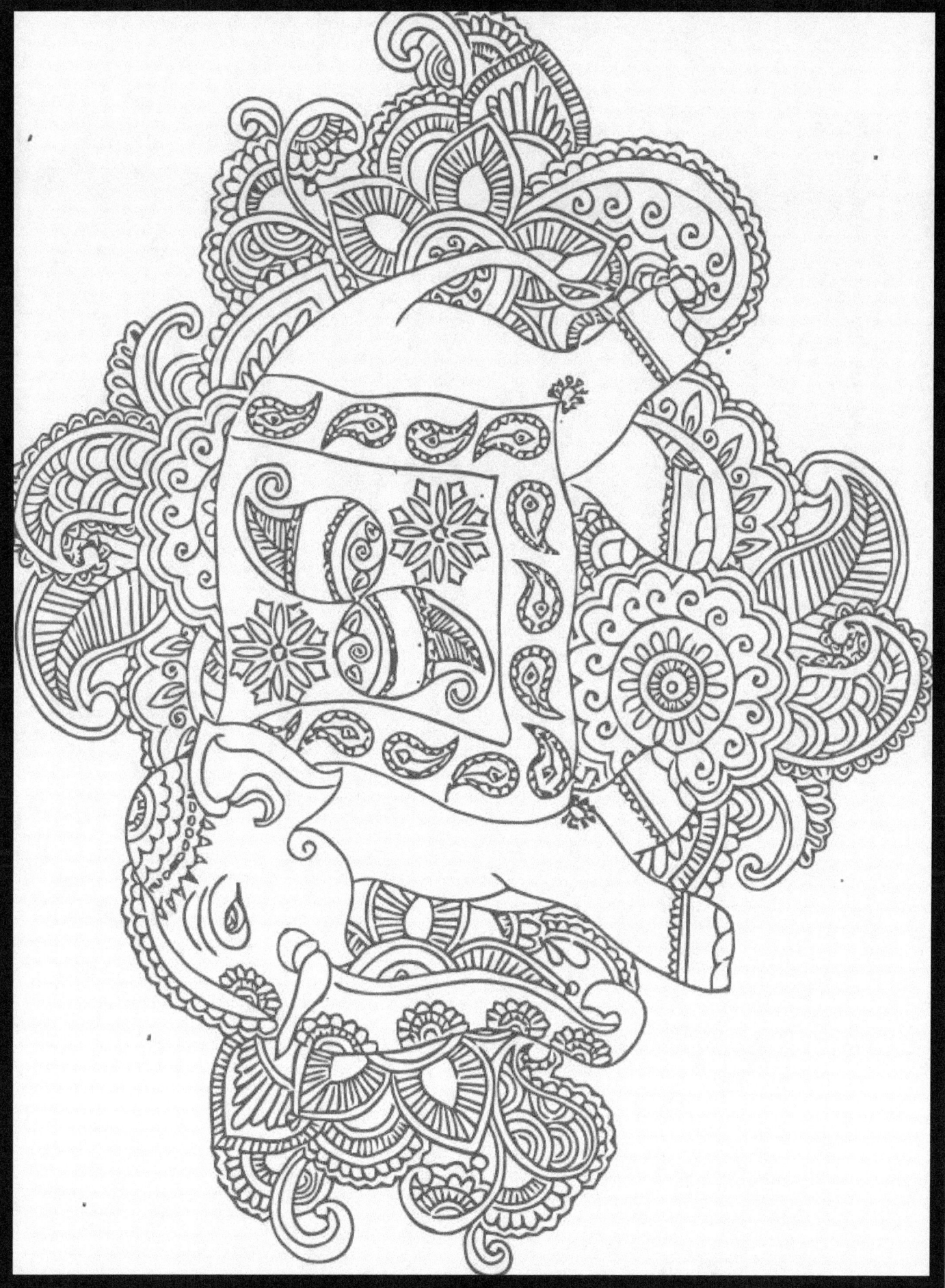

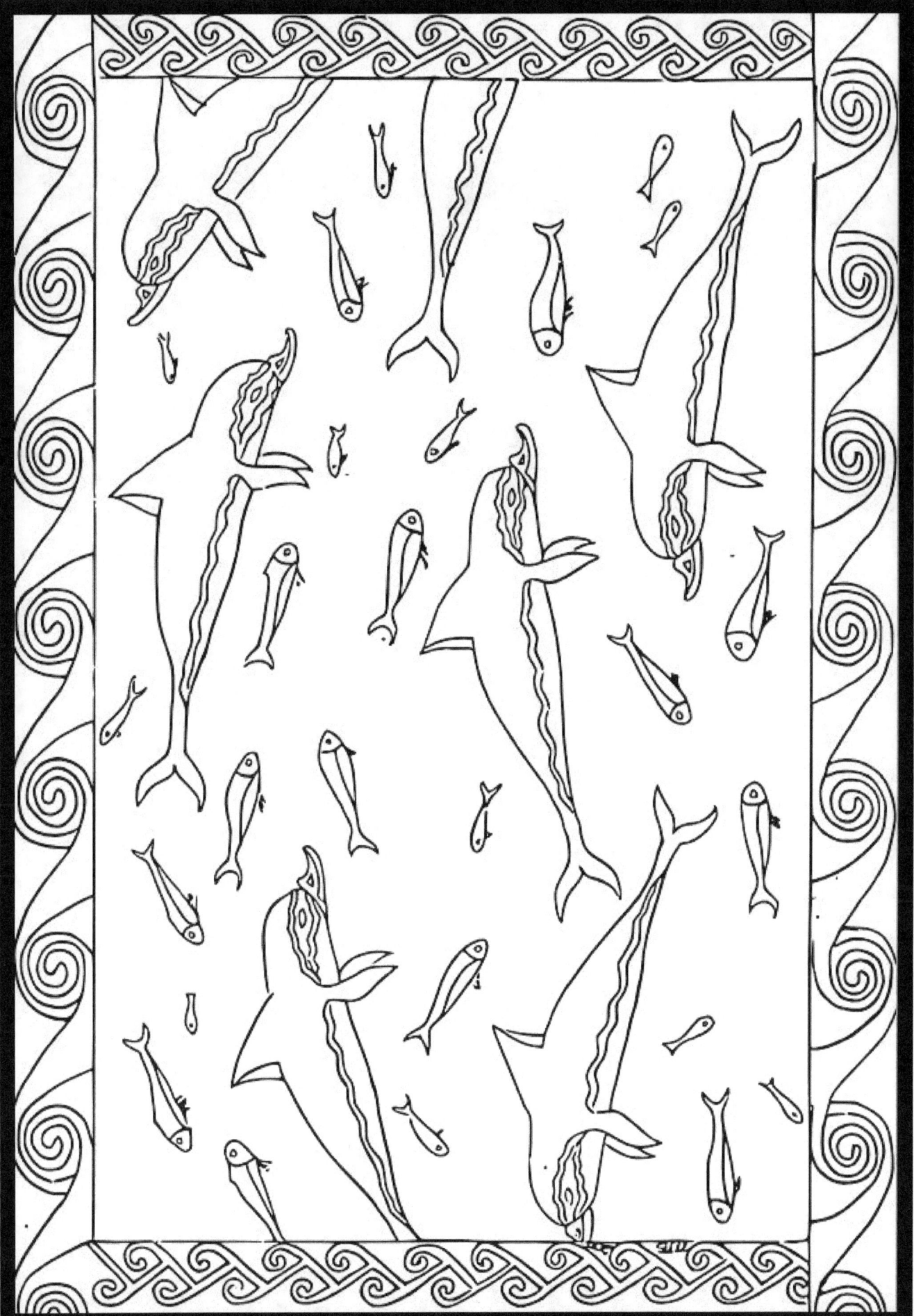

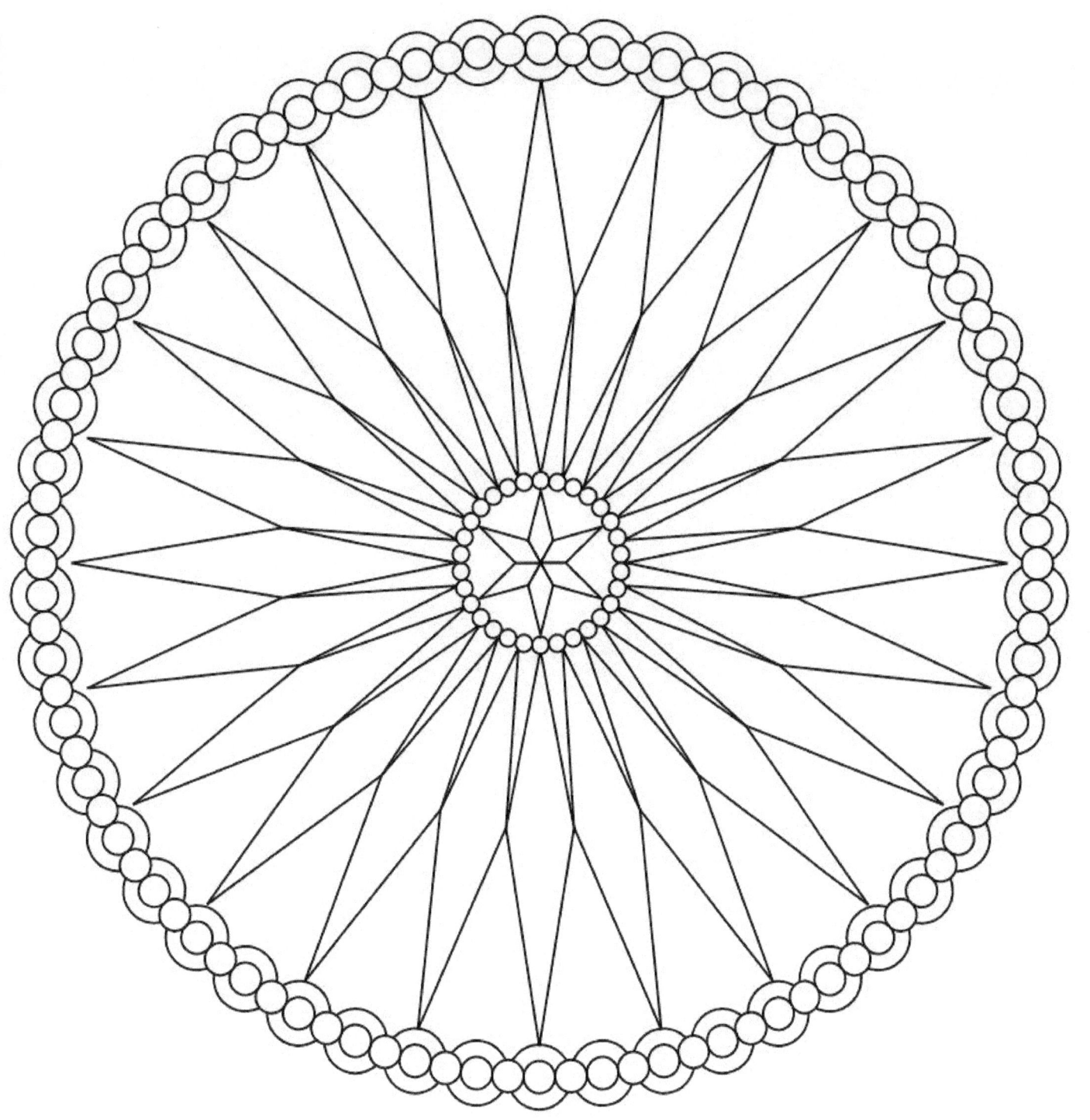

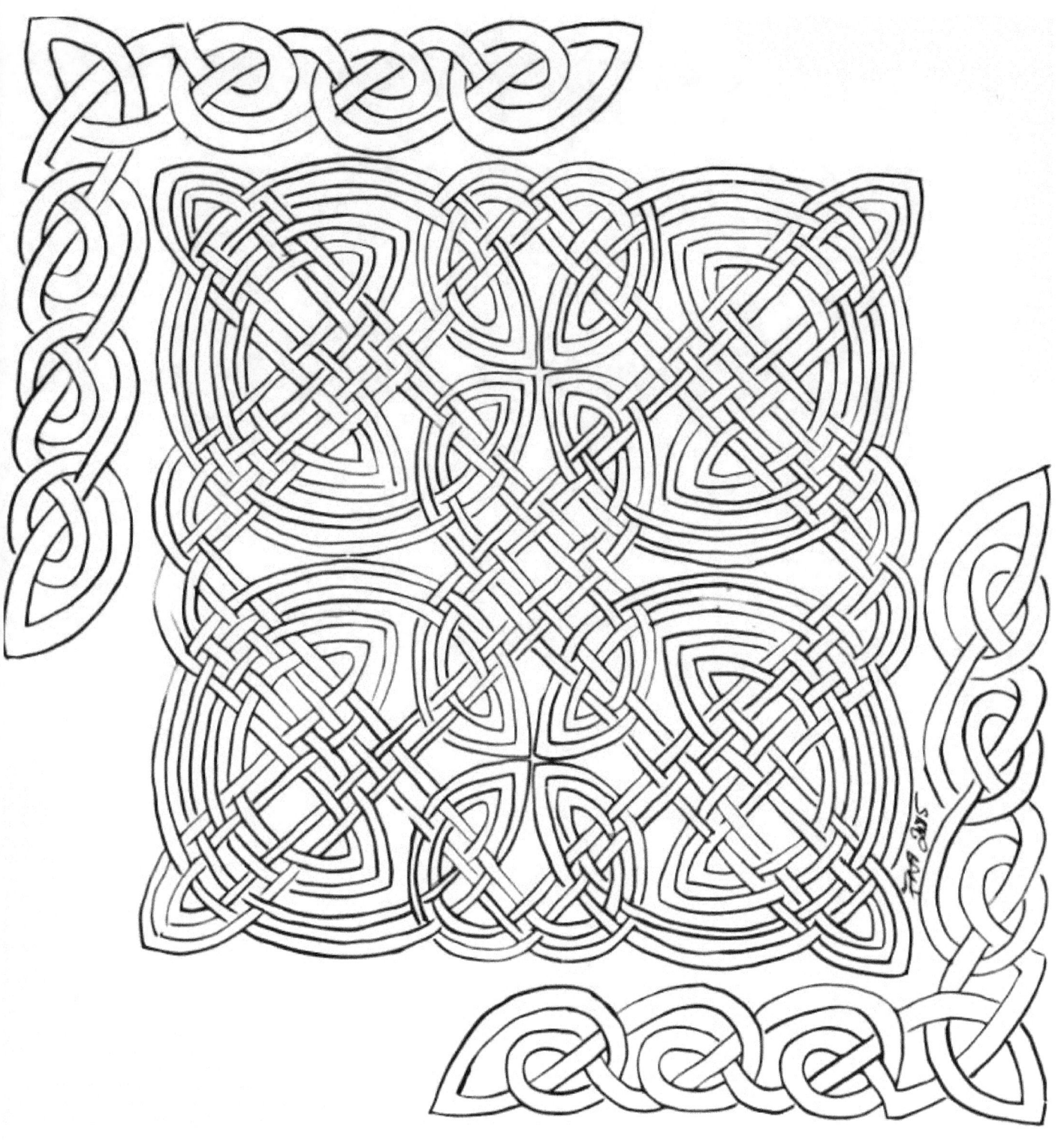

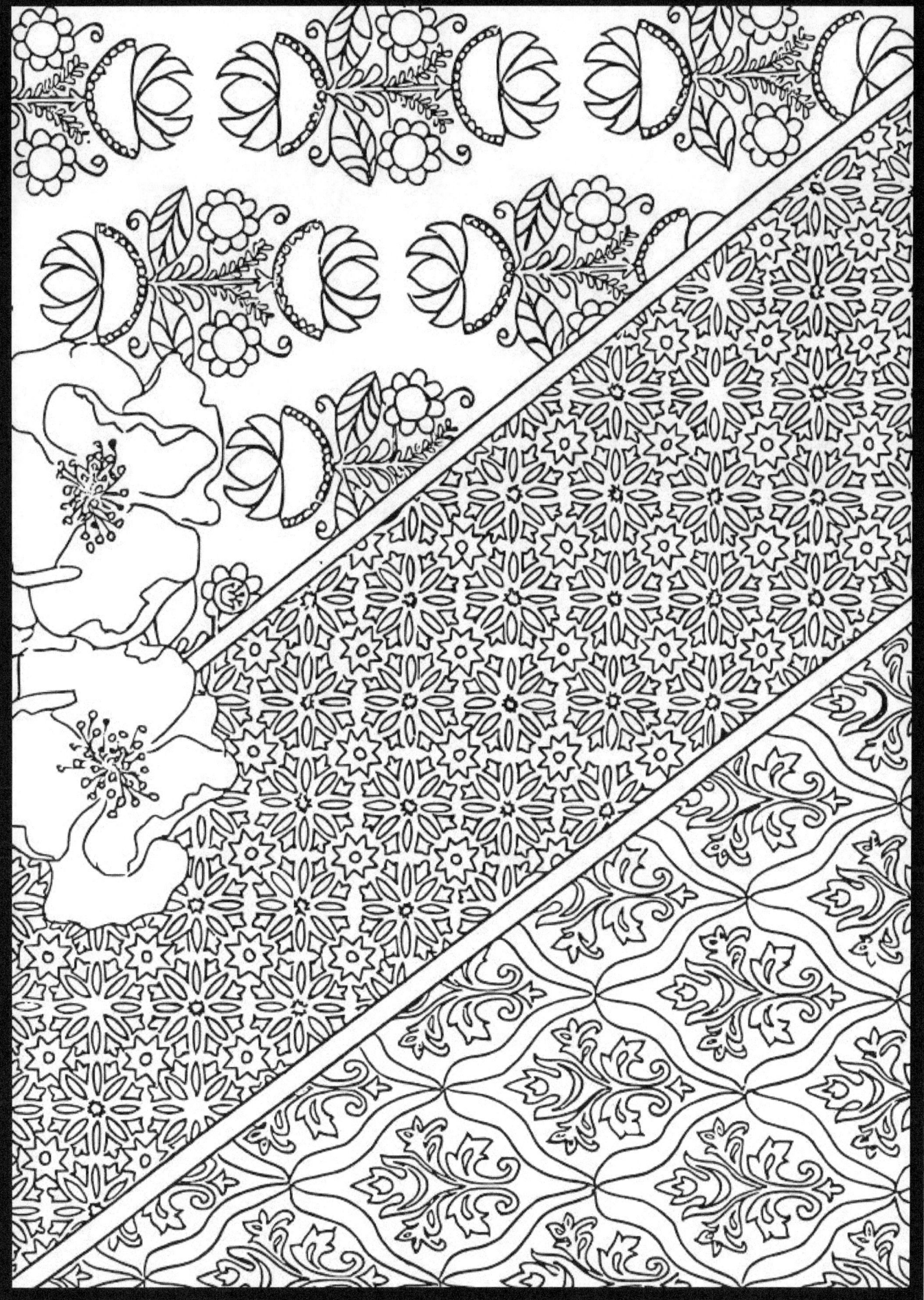

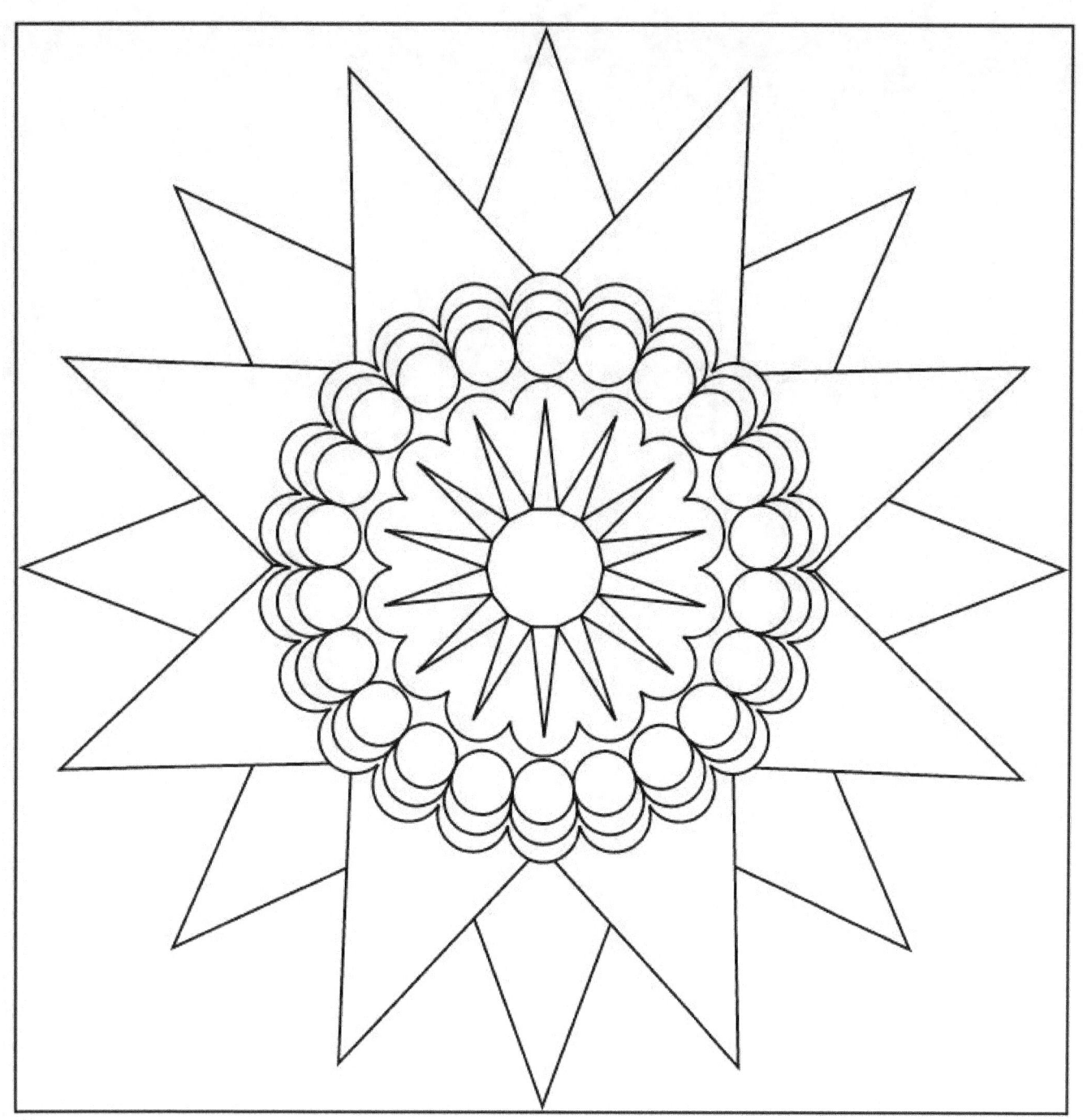

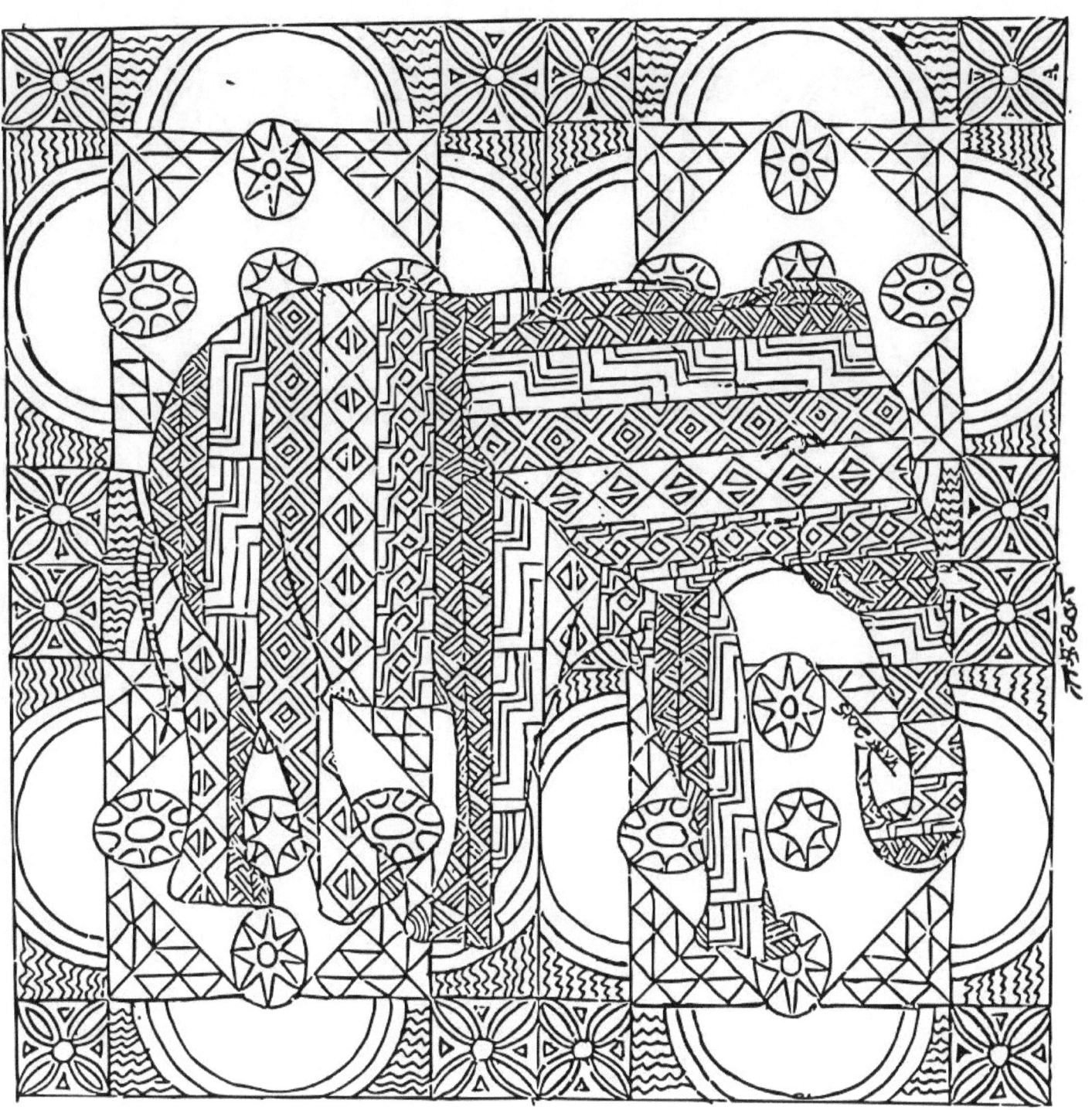